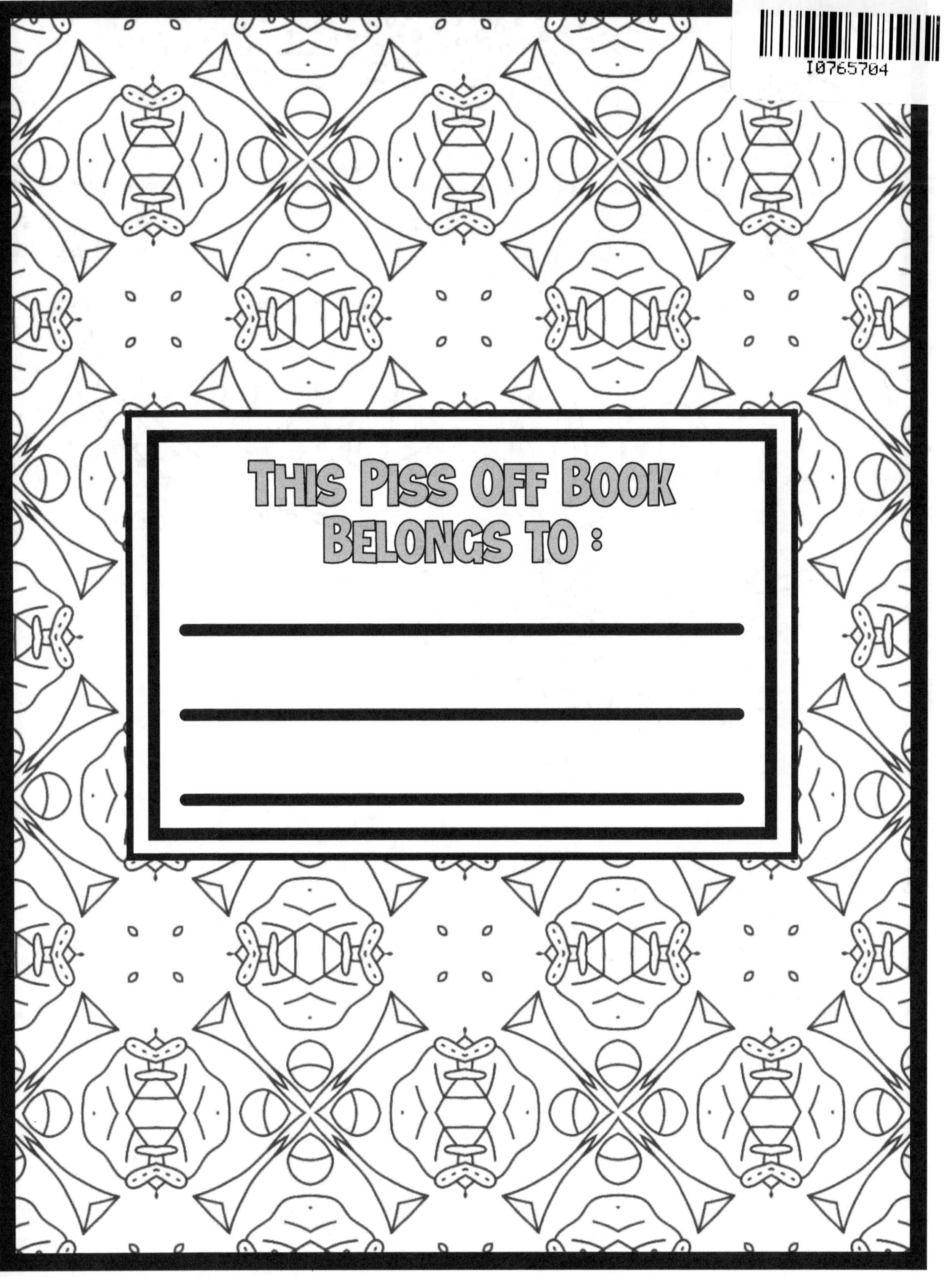

This Piss Off Book
Belongs to :

Copyright © 2020 Logan Anderson

First Printing, 2020

Triangle House Media LLC
Titusville, Florida
32780

Trianglehousemediallc.com

Those pants look
Uncomfortable
Take them off

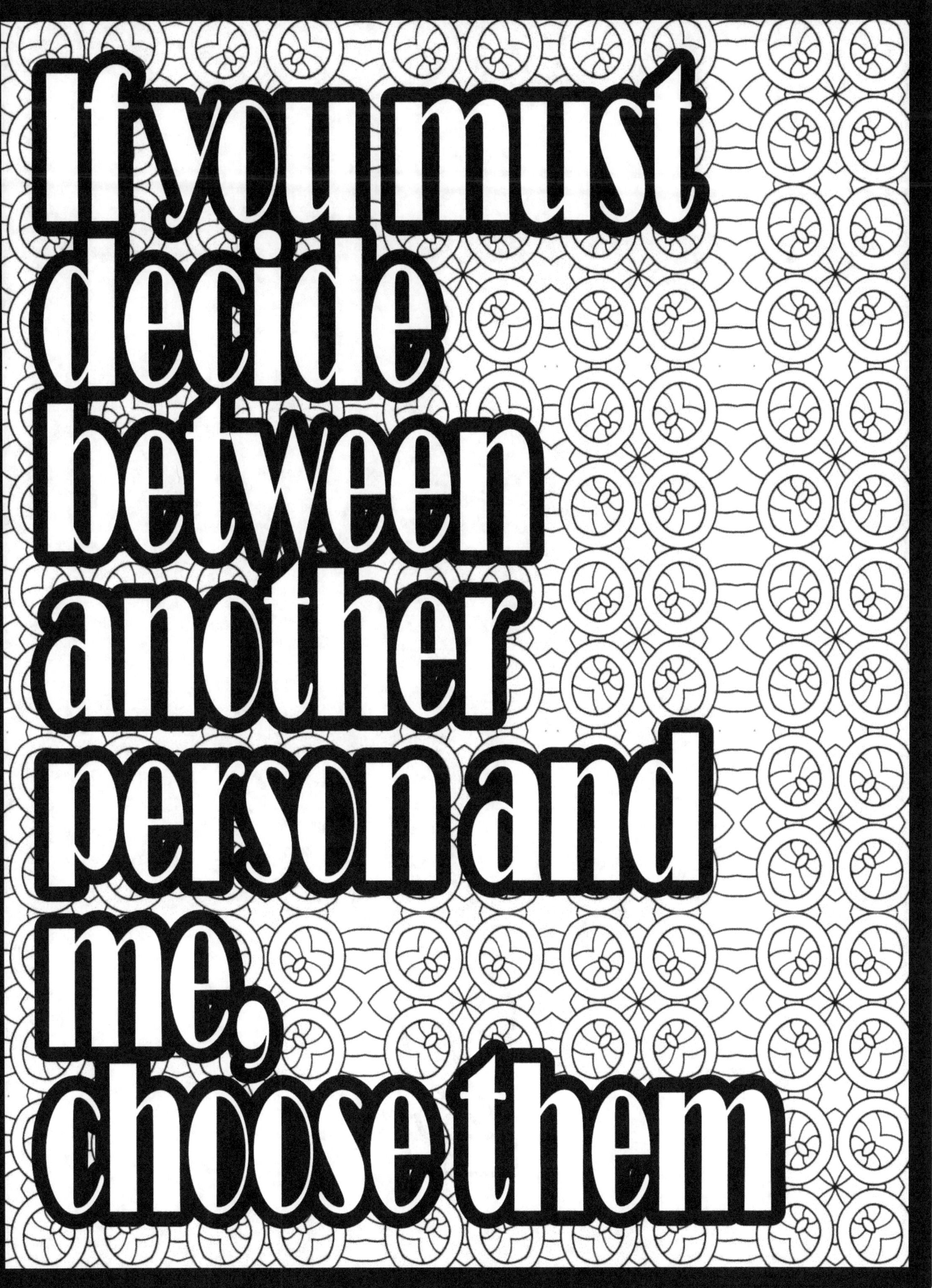

If you must decide between another person and me, choose them

2

There is a reason people only sleep with you once

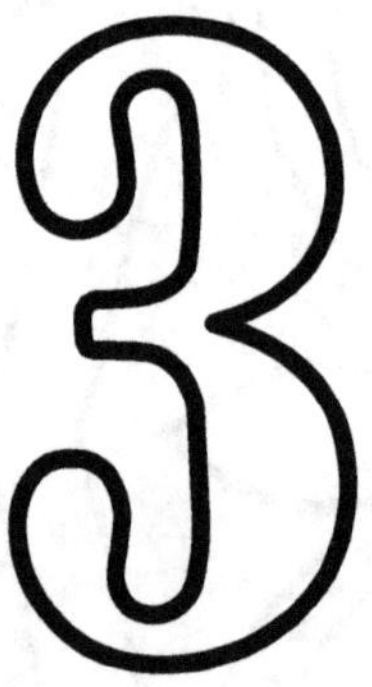

Relationship Status:
Single
Taken
Not Falling for that shit again

If you're
sneaky
and you
know it,
you're a
CHEAT!

5

Butt Stuff

ATTENTION
WHORE

7

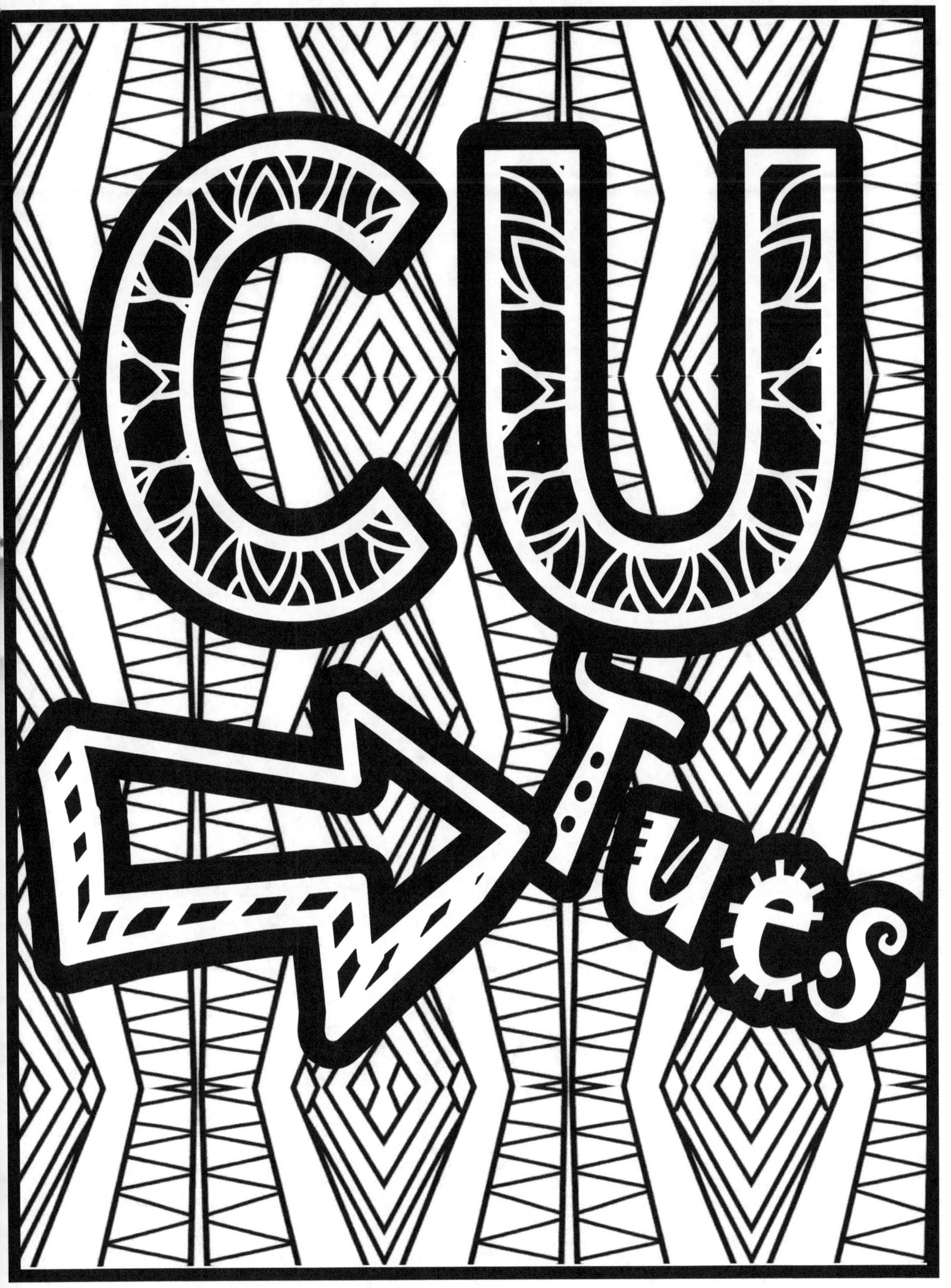

CU
Tues

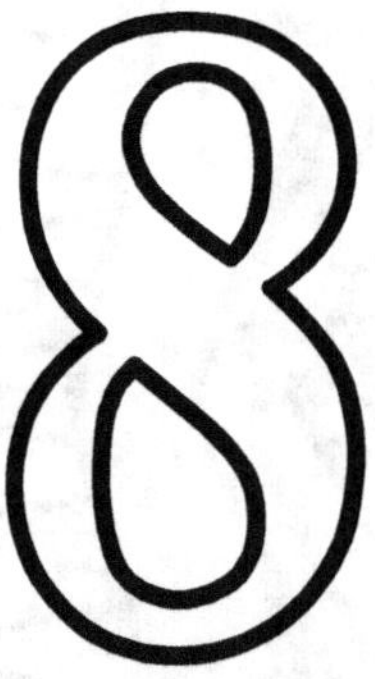

I'm Free

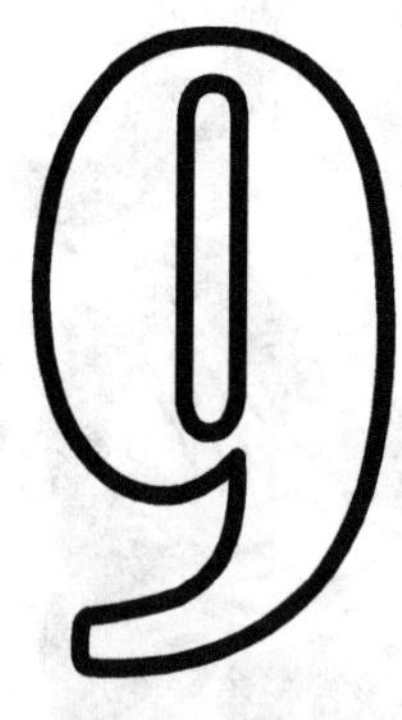

be
your
self

10

Communication
is
KEY

WHAT DO YOU WANT TO EAT?

Damnit

12

Fuck
You
Very
Much

13

14

I should have listened to my mother

15

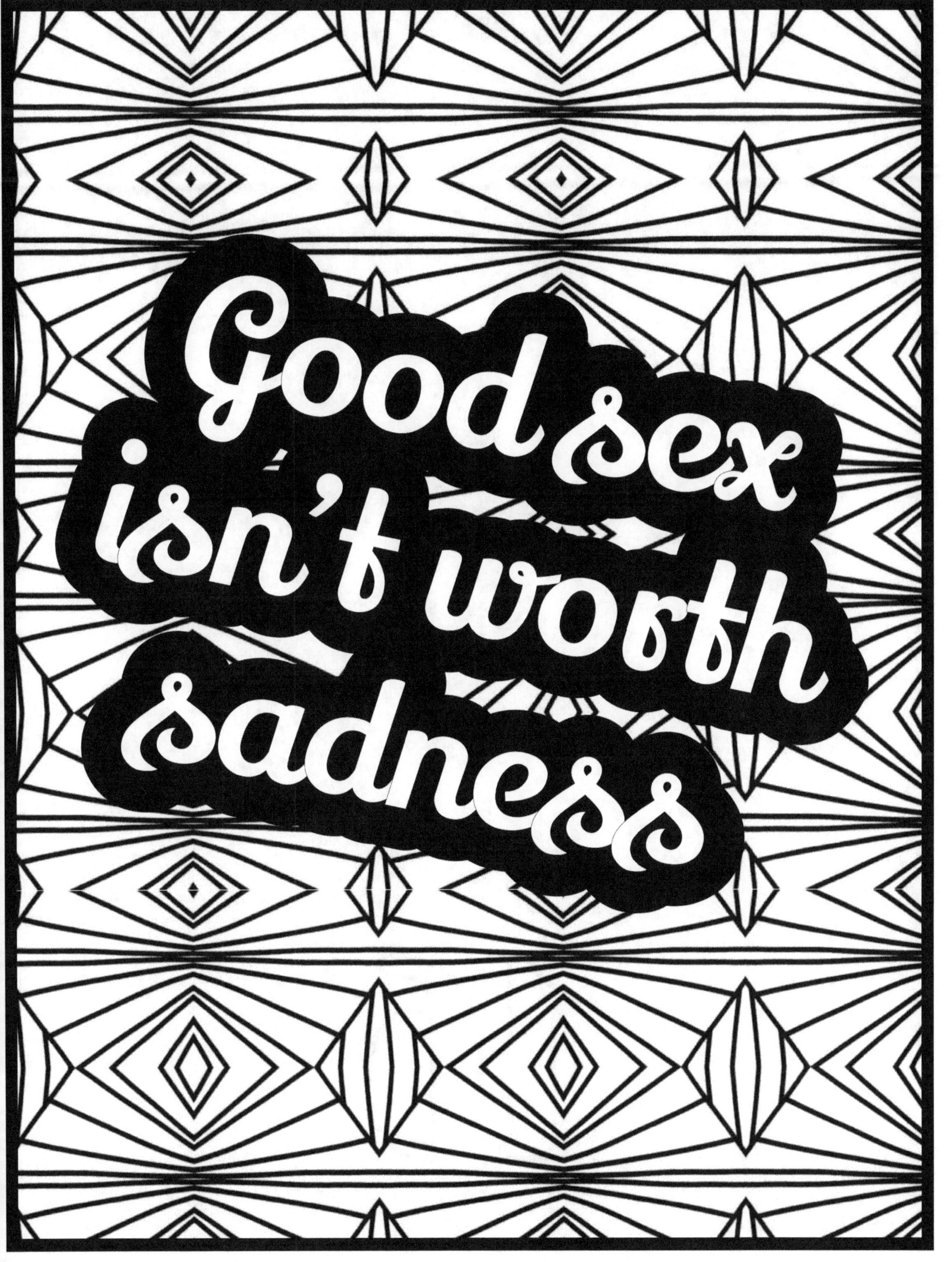

Good sex isn't worth sadness

16

I shaved my legs for this?

17

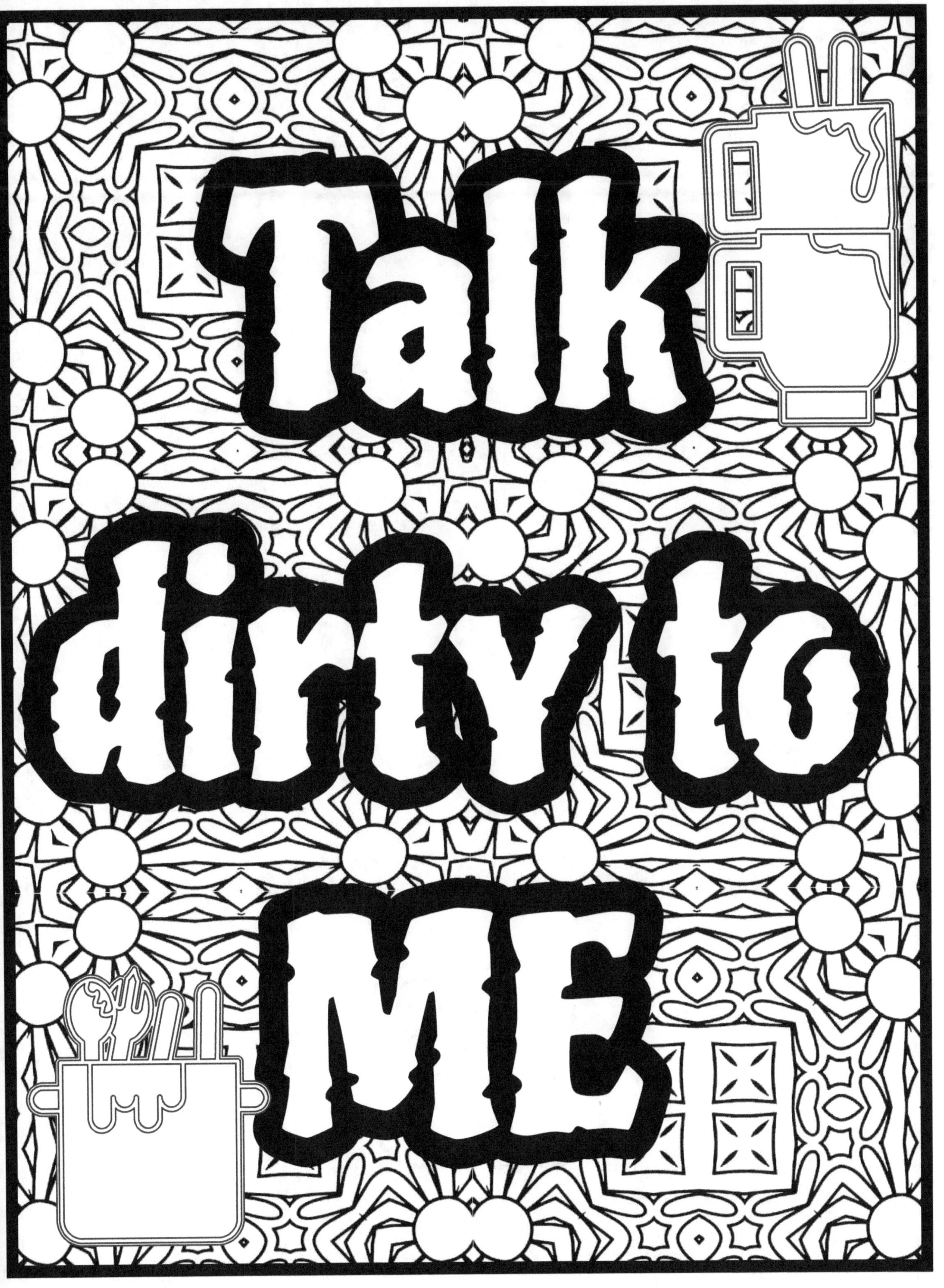
Talk
dirty to
ME

18

I faked it, every time

19

I HATE MEN.

Never mind...
He texted back

20

I LOVE YOU
LIKE
KANYE
LOVES
KANYE

21

Break
my Bed,
Not my
Heart.

22

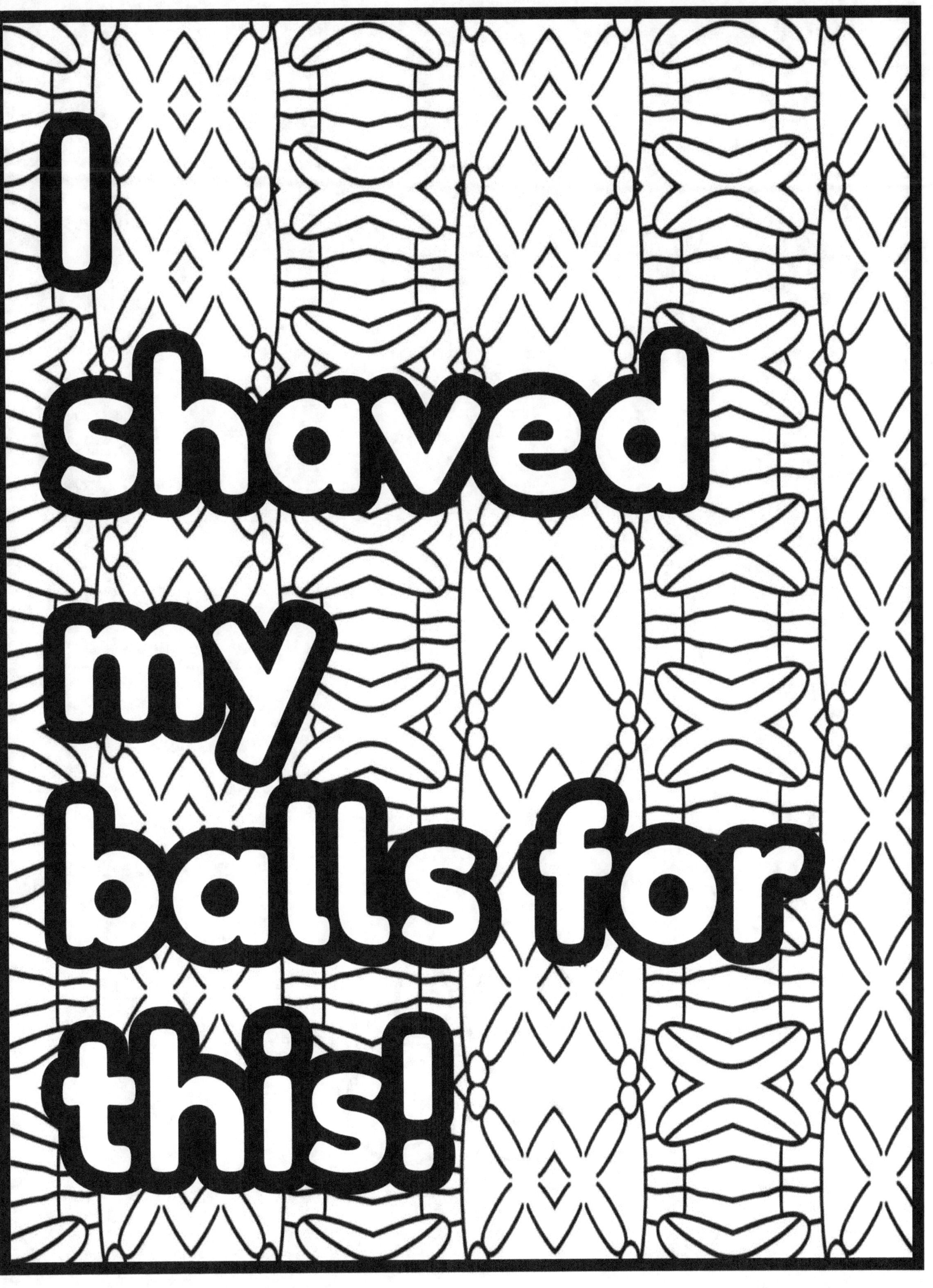

I shaved my balls for this!

23

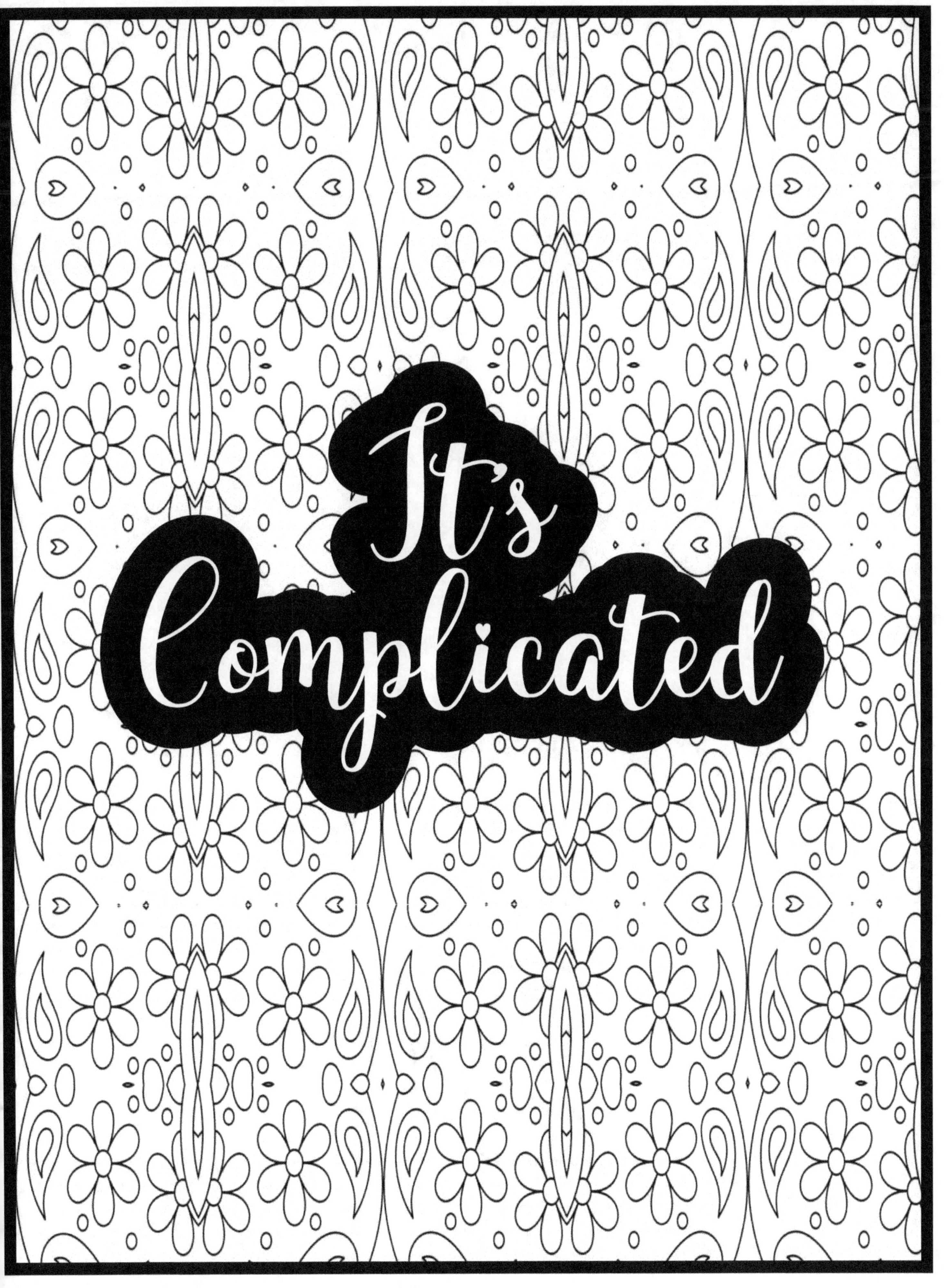
It's
Complicated

24

DIRTY
FUCKING
SLUT

25

FUCK
WIT

26

PISS
OFF

27

Pull my
hair,
don't
try my
patience

28

DO
WHAT
YOU
LOVE

29

I need
better
friends

30

MILF

31

I FUCK
LIKE A
PORN
STAR

32

Two Choices: Be Right or Be Happy

33

I wish
you would
grow the
fuck up

34

I KNOW WHY YOU ARE SINGLE

35

I miss you

36

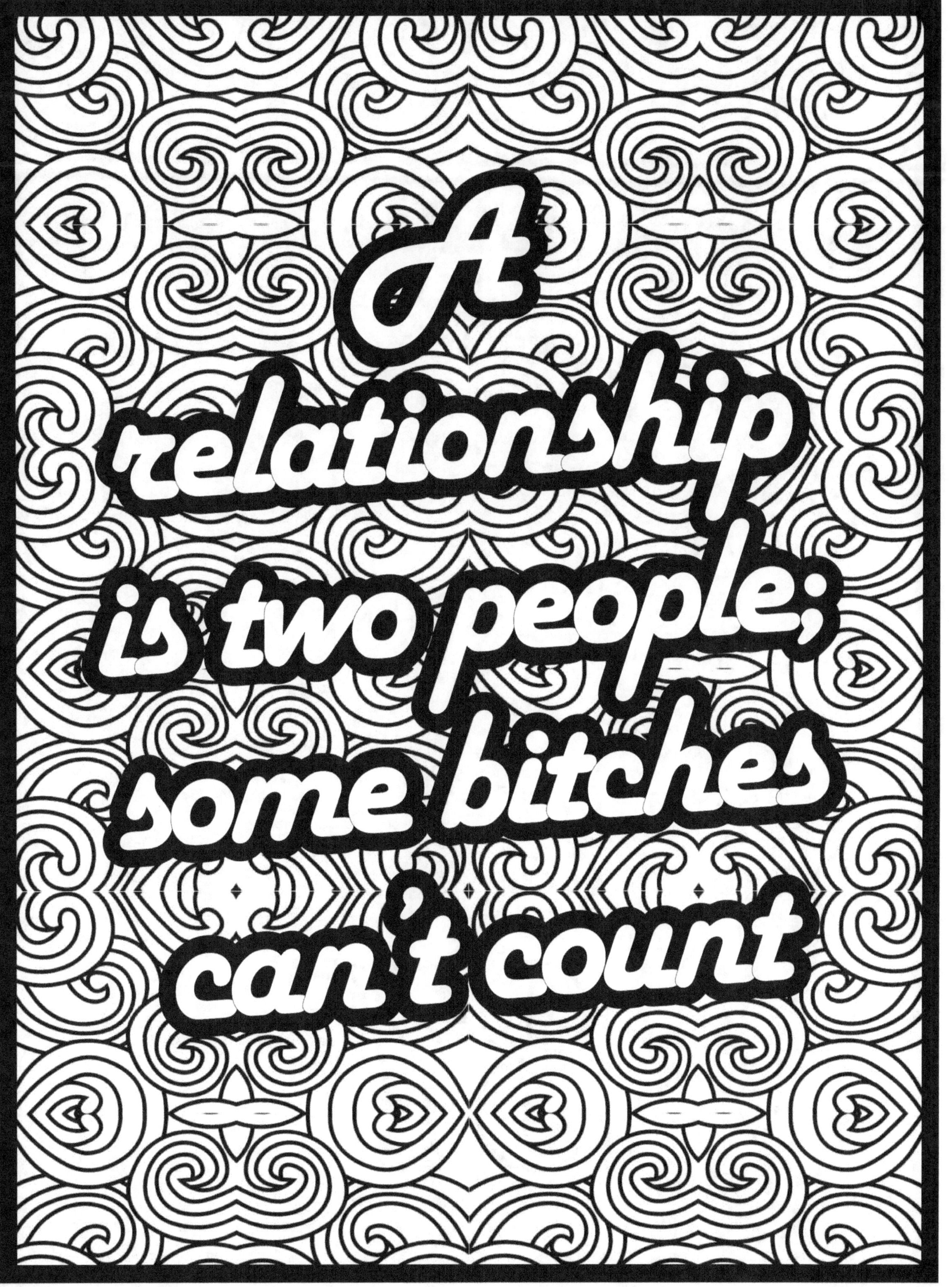

A
relationship
is two people;
some bitches
can't count

37

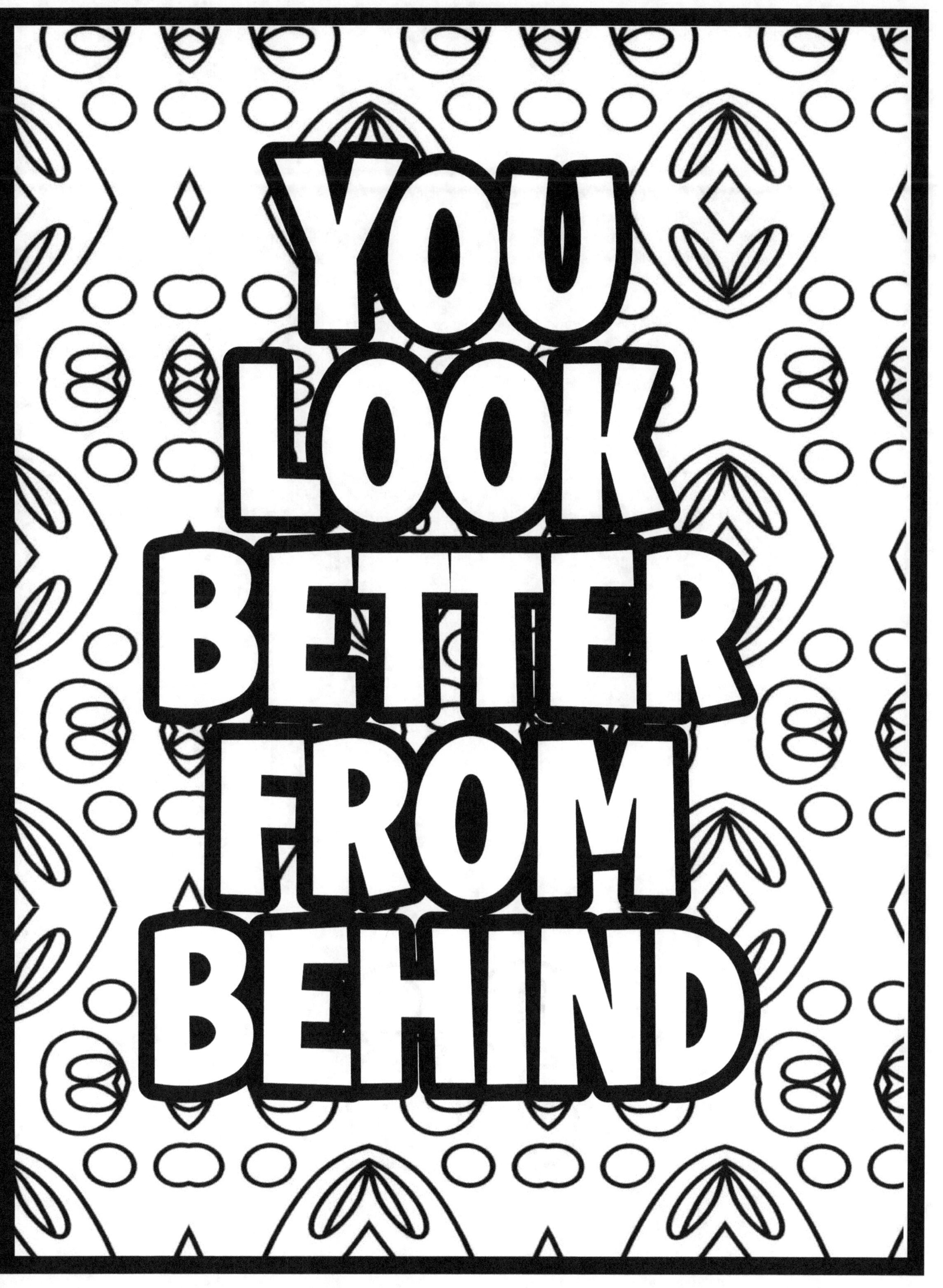

YOU
LOOK
BETTER
FROM
BEHIND

38

Be
brave

39

BITCH

40

Smile

41

All you need is:
LINGERIE
SAFEWORD
VODKA
HEELS

42

choose
joy

43

yes
you
can

44

Live
without
Regrets

45

You make my

mustache

TINGLE

46

You
can
Do it

47

APPARENTLY
we are
TROUBLE
WHEN WE ARE
together
WHO KNEW!

48

My love is like a candle. Forget me, and I will burn your fucking house down

49

YOU ARE THE
SALSA
OF MY
TACO

50